MY ROADMAP

ALSO BY SAM BRACKEN AND ECHO GARRETT

My Orange Duffel Bag:
A Journey to Radical Change

MY ROADMAP

a personal guide to balance,
power, and purpose by the authors
of **My Orange Duffel Bag**

Sam Bracken and Echo Garrett

CROWN ARCHETYPE / NEW YORK

Published in the United States by Crown Archetype, an imprint of the
Crown Publishing Group, a division of Random House, Inc., New York.

www.crownpublishing.com

Crown Archetype with colophon is a trademark of Random House, Inc.

I AM exercise on p. 38 used with permission of Cindy Hunsinger, CPPC, founder of
GUIDE Pointe, LLC and coaching director of Orange Duffel Bag Foundation.

Library of Congress Cataloging-in-Publication Data
Bracken, Sam.
My roadmap: a personal guide to balance, power, and purpose/
by Sam Bracken and Echo Garrett.—1st ed.
1. Goal (Psychology) 2. Self-actualization (Psychology)
3. Love. 4. Gratitude. 5. Bracken, Sam. I. Garrett, Echo. II. Title
BF505.G6B73 2012
158—dc23   2012003755

ISBN 978-0-307-95586-9

Printed in the United States of America

BOOK DESIGN BY ELINA D. NUDELMAN
COVER DESIGN BY LAURA DUFFY
PHOTOGRAPHS BY KEVIN GARRETT (PAGES 9, 46, 63, 87, 99, 115, 135)

10 9 8 7 6 5 4 3 2 1

First Edition

For our children:

Beau, Ben, Jake, and Hannah Bracken; Caleb and Connor Garrett

And for our loving spouses:

Kim Bracken and Kevin Garrett

With special thanks to Richard Becker, MAEd, director/founder of Chrysalis Experiential Academy; Orange Duffel Bag Foundation (ODBF) Director of Coaching Cindy Hunsinger, CPCC; ODBF Program Director Susan Brown, ED.S., CATCC; and ODBF board member Brent Jorgensen, MAEd

WHAT'S INSIDE

READY . . . SET . . . GO!

"It's been a

long time coming,

but I know

a change is

gonna come."

ARTIST-SONGWRITER
SAM COOKE

7 RULES FOR THE ROAD

for My Journey to Radical Change

THE STARTING POINT
Sam's Story

When I made the decision as a thirteen-year-old that I wanted to change my life, I had no idea how to do it.

I lived in an abusive, drug- and alcohol-fueled household on the fringe of Las Vegas. I didn't have role models beyond the motorcycle gang members and mobsters that my mom and stepdad allowed to hang around our family. I was in special-education classes in school until eighth grade, when a caring teacher figured out that I needed glasses.

In the face of those barriers and many others, I did my best to find affirmations to encourage myself. I looked for inspiration anywhere I could find it: positive music, words that had inspiring messages, beautiful pictures from magazines, uplifting books, and movies about overcomers.

I set some goals for myself: I wanted to be a professional football player and a lawyer. I really didn't know what a lawyer did, but from watching television I thought it looked like a pretty good job. Lawyers wore nice suits and appeared to have plenty of money. Because of that goal, I knew I needed to do well in school, so I decided that in high school I was going to make straight A's.

Then my plans ran headlong into the harsh realities of my life. My mom abandoned me when I was fifteen to be sort of a den mother to the Hessian motorcycle gang. That was a big roadblock. Despite being homeless, I stayed in school, worked any job I could find, went to track and football practice, and focused on my goals.

I began to formulate a path out of the life of abuse and craziness I'd been born into. Eventually I earned a full-ride football scholarship to the Georgia Institute of Technology in Atlanta. When I left Las Vegas for Atlanta, I packed my meager belongings into an orange duffel bag along with all my hopes and dreams for the future.

Despite the incredible accomplishment of landing a scholarship at one of the nation's most academically challenging schools, I still continued to wrestle with how to make lasting changes in my life—how to get where I wanted to go.

My life crumbled when I suffered seemingly career-ending shoulder injuries after my freshman year. I had surgery on both shoulders, and nobody thought I'd ever play football again. I was tempted to feel sorry for myself and to give up.

I tried to rehabilitate my injured body, working hard to strengthen my shoulders by running and swimming and lifting weights like a man possessed, but I wasn't making much progress. That's when I went to one of my trusted mentors, Coach Bill Curry, for help. I explained my frustration, and he gave me the answer that launched me on the journey I'm still on today.

Coach Curry told me to get a binder, make four tabs, and label them *physical, mental, emotional,* and *spiritual.* "Then write down a personal inventory in each section of where you are right now," he instructed. "Next, take a page and write down what you want to accomplish in each section in the next year. Write down just a few things, so you won't get overwhelmed. On the next page in each section write down a compelling reason to accomplish your goals. Finally, write down how you will get it done.

"Once you do that, read what you have written every day for about fifteen minutes. Then after two weeks rip out the page that described where you were. Every day positively embrace what you want, why you want it, and how and when you will get it. **Affirm your success in each area and keep working hard. Know that I am here for you if you need anything."**

I did exactly what he said. That notebook changed everything. It allowed me to formulate a clear vision for what I wanted in every major area of my life. Over the years, I expanded on the germ of that notebook idea. I realized that there were seven things that helped me get out of poverty and abuse and develop into the person I was meant to be. I chronicled my journey, along with the 7 *Rules for the Road* that helped me change, in *My Orange Duffel Bag: A Journey to Radical Change.* And now with *My Roadmap*, I hope to help you on your own personal journey to radical change.

My Roadmap can help you find meaning, purpose, and vision in your life. It will also help you:

• Learn how to set and accomplish important goals

• Understand and make good choices that will lead to positive changes in your life

• Creatively work through and tell "your story"

• Practice an attitude of gratitude

In the first part, we'll travel the 7 *Rules for the Road* together. By the end, you'll have discovered what really matters to you, identified your greatest talents and gifts, learned how to navigate roadblocks and enjoy detours, and developed a clear plan for getting you where you want to be in life. At the end of each chapter, you'll find two blank pages where you can record additional thoughts that the exercises spark.

The second section is your own journal goal book like the one I create for myself every year. The work you put into the first section will help you identify where you need to grow in each area: physical, mental, emotional, and spiritual. In the second section you'll record goals in each area and measure your progress. I use my journal goal book to inspire me, and paste in it uplifting sayings and pictures that move me. I draw in it. I dream. I doodle. I hope you'll use this space in the same way. Get creative. This book is all about you.

The third section, called *My Life*, is a place for you to write down what you are grateful for in your life. Gratitude is the final *Rule for the Road*, because it's a key element in any successful journey, and the *My Life* section is designed for you to express your hopes, dreams, and joys. As you fill this section, focus on the future and the positive outcomes this book will help you achieve.

I review my roadmap every day to be sure I'm on the right path, and my goal books from previous years have become keepsakes that allow me to see how far I've come. It's my hope that this journal becomes as indispensable to you.

Enjoy your journey to radical change.

—*Sam Bracken*

> "A creative man is motivated by the desire to achieve, not by the desire to beat others."
>
> —AYN RAND

look around

Take a long, hard look at exactly where you are in life right now.

The desire to be different is where change begins. Change cannot happen without a fierce desire that burns in your heart, mind, soul, and gut.

Right off the bat, let me tell you that the odds of making a lasting radical change in your life are stacked against you. Scary fact: Even when their lives are at stake, most people refuse to budge from what often proves to be the deadliest place on earth: the comfort zone.

In fact, only one out of every nine people acts on the desire for something new and different and radically changes behavior.

Be that ONE to change.

You may be asking yourself . . .

WHY CHANGE? CHANGE IS THE ONE CONSTANT IN OUR WORLD.

What are the benefits of changing and growing constantly?

- Boosted confidence (self-esteem)

- A greater sense of accomplishment

- Increased knowledge and awareness (knowledge is power)

- Superior ability to adapt, learn, and grow to succeed in life regardless of environment

- Heightened capacity to prioritize life's demands

- Better ability to make important life decisions

- Dramatic improvement in the quality of your life

- Maximizing your potential

- Achieving your dreams

What gets in the way of change? What are the barriers or obstacles? Why do most people resist change?

- A stuck mind-set. We SEE no need to change. We get stuck in the comfort zone or become paralyzed with fear.

- Lack of clarity on WHAT to change. Living in the fog.

- Don't know HOW to change. No proven process for change.

- Missing a compelling REASON to change. No motivation to change.

- No real ACCOUNTABILITY from people who love you.

What will happen if you CHOOSE NOT to embrace change?

- Left behind
- Make little or no progress
- Unprepared to meet life's challenges

RADICAL CHANGE IS POWER THAT POWER LIVES IN YOUR SOUL.

The course is set for radical change in your life when these three things collide:

- You have a bold vision of your future.
- You're not happy with where you are or the pain you feel.
- You get in touch emotionally with how your actions or inactions are negatively affecting you or someone you love.

When you are willing to work on changing yourself, you are ready to change your future.

"Take the first step in faith. You don't have to see the whole staircase, just take the first step."

-Dr. Martin Luther King, Jr.

TRAVEL TIP 151332

In your current state, you are perfectly aligned to get the same old results out of life you are getting right now. If you want new or better results, you must first change your thoughts, because your thoughts DRIVE your behavior. You cannot control other people and you may not be able to control your environment. But you can control your thoughts and how you respond to people, the events in your life, and your environment. What is insanity? Albert Einstein defined insanity as doing the same thing over and over again and expecting a different result.

MAPPING MY COURSE

You can't get where you want to go if you don't know where you are. So where are you in your life right now? Take twenty minutes and tell your story on the following pages. Feel free to write a few paragraphs, or a poem, or draw a timeline, highlighting the most significant events in your life (good and bad). Do whatever feels most comfortable and helps you to be as candid as possible. Don't sugarcoat the truth. This is the time to be completely honest with yourself about where your life is headed. And if you don't like the direction, understand that the time has come to change it.

Here are some questions that might help you get started: What are some of your earliest memories? Achievements? Challenges? Who are the significant people in your life? Think about sights, sounds, and smells that you vividly recall. What events are they connected to?

Or flip through this book and find a quote that speaks to you, and then write a few paragraphs about how it relates to your life.

"*Don't let the darkness of the past cover the brightness of the future.*"

-Unknown

"What makes the engine go? Desire, desire, desire." -Stanley Kunitz

WHAT'S IN YOUR BAG?

I carried my hopes, dreams, and desires with me to college in an orange duffel bag. You may not realize it, but you have a bag, too, and the contents of your bag can help take you to where you want to go.

Examine the contents of your bag. Look back on what you just wrote. Did you list any of your hopes, dreams, and desires for how you'd like your life to be? Were there things about yourself or your life that made you unhappy or frustrated, or that you wanted to change? How do you want to change your life—your actions, your thoughts, your condition?

Don't edit yourself. Just let your thoughts flow.

Now use the four categories below to help organize what you'd like to change. These four areas cover what makes a complete human being. As a teen, I valued myself only for what I could do physically on the football field. My college football coach taught me that I needed to think of myself as a whole person and set goals in all four areas in order to lead a balanced life. Often we tend to focus on just one or two of these areas, which leads to us being out of balance.

 PHYSICAL/BODY: What would you like to change about your body, appearance, or health?

_____

_____

_____

_____

_____

_____

_____

_____

_____

_____

_____

_____

_____

MENTAL/MIND: What would you like to change about the way you think about yourself, your circumstances, or others? Do you want to improve your mental health? Your intellectual powers? Your educational pursuits?

_____

_____

_____

_____

_____

_____

_____

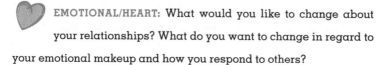 **EMOTIONAL/HEART:** What would you like to change about your relationships? What do you want to change in regard to your emotional makeup and how you respond to others?

_____

_____

_____

_____

_____

_____

_____

SPIRITUAL/SOUL: What do you want to change about your inner self? How can you be more in touch with your soul?

_____

_____

_____

_____

_____

_____

_____

PHYSICAL/BODY: Why is it important to change or accomplish something in this area right now? Why do you want to be different?

_____

_____

_____

_____

_____

_____

_____

MENTAL/MIND: Why is it important to change or accomplish something in this area right now? Why do you want to be different?

_____

_____

_____

_____

_____

_____

_____

EMOTIONAL/HEART: Why is it important to change or accomplish something in this area right now? Why do you want to be different?

_____

_____

_____

_____

_____

_____

_____

SPIRITUAL/SOUL: Why is it important to change or accomplish something in this area right now? Why do you want to be different?

_____

_____

_____

_____

_____

_____

 PHYSICAL/BODY: What motivates you to be different in this area?

_____

_____

_____

_____

_____

_____

_____

MENTAL/MIND: What motivates you to be different in this area?

_____

_____

_____

_____

_____

_____

 EMOTIONAL/HEART: What motivates you to be different in this area?

_____

_____

_____

_____

_____

_____

_____

_____

SPIRITUAL/SOUL: What motivates you to be different in this area?

_____

_____

_____

_____

_____

_____

_____

What goals will mean the most to you once you've accomplished them in each of these areas?

Many people I've met have been motivated by a negative emotion like fear or anger. However, when the negative fuels your actions, you eventually flame out. For example, if you have a heart attack due to being overweight and decide to make lifestyle changes, which would motivate you more: a fear of dying or a desire to live a full and joyous life? Fear can be a powerful motivator for a little while, but for the long haul, you need to focus on the positive. Love conquers fear. Let love be the WHY behind each of your goals.

PHYSICAL/BODY: List your goals in order of importance to you.

_____

_____

_____

_____

_____

_____

_____

MENTAL/MIND: List your goals in order of importance to you.

_____

_____

_____

_____

_____

_____

_____

EMOTIONAL/HEART: List your goals in order of importance to you.

 SPIRITUAL/SOUL: List your goals in order of importance to you.

Use the next two pages to record how "Rule 1: Desire" impacts your
thinking.

"*The starting point of all achievement is desire.*"   -Napoleon Hill

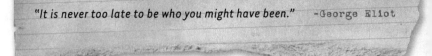

"*It is never too late to be who you might have been.*" -George Eliot

"The truth is that our finest moments are most likely to occur when we are feeling deeply uncomfortable, unhappy, or unfulfilled. For it is only in such moments, propelled by our discomfort, that we are likely to step out of our ruts and start searching for different ways or truer answers."

-M. SCOTT PECK

AWARENESS

RULE

find your ticket
to ride

What are you good at? That is your ticket to ride. Take a moment and really think about it. To get to where you want to go, you've got to have a destination in mind and a ticket to ride.

IGNORANCE IS THE ENEMY OF CHOICE AND CHANGE.

Knowing what you are good at takes self-awareness. You must be able to identify what you are good at in order to move ahead on your journey.

So how do you find your ticket?

Here are three ways:

• Experience that Aha! moment—that divine instant when you suddenly know what your talent is and how to get your ticket.

- Listen to someone wise who cares about you and who knows you well—a mentor, friend, family member, teacher, or coach—and ask that person to point out your ticket.

- Earn your ticket by learning—explore ideas through reading books and find topics that spark your curiosity. Examine the lives of others whom you admire.

Claiming your ticket may not be easy.

You may have misplaced it.

Sometimes you lose your ticket.

Your ticket may not look like what you expected:

Sometimes it is stamped for the wrong destination.

Or the price of it may appear too steep to pay.

Do whatever it takes to get that golden ticket.

MAPPING MY COURSE

Find your ticket to ride. What are you good at?

Make a list of your strengths. Explore your passions and talents. As you write about what your natural gifts are, be willing to consider some areas that you might not have immediately thought of before.

If you get stuck, ask a trusted friend or mentor what talents and strengths he or she sees in you.

"Don't be pushed by your problems. Be led by your dreams."

-George Lorimer

_____

_____

_____

_____

_____

_____

Now that you've listed your greatest strengths and talents, what will your ticket cost you? My ticket cost me lots of lost sleep, intense work, and some relationships with family members who weren't safe.

Will you have to learn and do anything new to get your ticket? I had to learn how to study and focus despite chaos. Are you willing to pay the price? A lot of times, we may say we want to move ahead, but we aren't willing to make the sacrifices to pay for our ticket. For example, you can be an analytical thinker and great at arguing your case and dream of being a trial attorney, but if you aren't willing to spend the years in law school and investing in that career path, then you won't be able to claim the ticket that would move you down that path.

Once you've found your ticket, hold on to it. Guard it like your life depends on it.

Use affirmations, positive images, written goals, and good music to drown out your critics. Maybe the loudest, most critical voice you hear is inside your own head, a whining messenger who bleats: "You can't, you won't, you shouldn't." DON'T LISTEN TO THAT VOICE!

As a ninth grader, Michael Jordan got cut from his high school basketball team. He worked out with the team anyway and made it the next year, going on to glory as one of the NBA's greatest players ever.

J. K. Rowling, a single mom who struggled with thoughts of suicide and who was on public assistance, racked up 129 rejections for *Harry Potter*. She believed in her writing when no one else did and refused to give up her dream. Now she's richer than the Queen of England and was named *Time*'s 2007 Person of the Year.

When Richard Branson, who has dyslexia, dropped out of school at age sixteen, the headmaster told his mom that her son would never amount to anything. Now a billionaire, Branson owns more than 100 different companies, including Virgin Atlantic Airways. He is deeply involved in efforts to fight world hunger and AIDS, as well as global warming, and was named 2007 Citizen of the Year by the United Nations.

All of these people determinedly held on to their ticket and kept their dream destination in sight—no matter what the critics said.

> "Today is life—the only life you are sure of. Make the most of today. Get interested in something. Shake yourself awake. Develop a hobby. Let the winds of enthusiasm sweep through you. Live today with gusto."
>
> –George Lorimer

MAPPING MY COURSE

Knowing that having a positive self-image is vital to your journey is one thing. Actually being positive and living that is another altogether. I know firsthand what a battle it is to squelch negative self-talk and put up a barrier between your brain and all the negativity surrounding you. What I'm asking you to do is hard, but it will help you take the high road and lead you to your dream destination.

Finish the sentence below with words that positively describe you. Write as many as you can think of. (Example: I am courageous. I am caring. I am optimistic. I am generous. I am helpful.)

I am

I am

I am

I am

I am

I am

I am

I am

I am

I am

I am

I am

Review this list often. Practice substituting a positive thought about one of your strengths whenever you are tempted to dwell on the negative and to combat negative feedback from those around you. My self-esteem was nonexistent. Early on, I carried around note cards, each with a positive word about myself and an encouraging quote or scripture to combat my inner critic. I got in the habit of using affirmations for living.

Write one sentence that sums up your special gift—your ticket to ride—and repeat it to yourself as often as needed. For example, mine was: "I am a great football player." Now it has become: "I am a prolific author, speaker, and producer committed to positively impacting the lives of millions."

_____

_____

_____

_____

_____

Now make yourself say the words:

I am AWESOME at _____

Do not soften the affirmation by saying:

I am OKAY at _____

Or even

I am GOOD at _____

Anyone who has achieved greatness in an area will tell you that using positive thoughts and visualizing yourself being where you want to be are essential to getting you there.

If you're having trouble identifying your special gift, find a champion and enlist that person's help. Write down your champion's name.

_____

Now I carry a rare coin from China that one of my best friends, Michael Simpson, presented to me, telling me that he gave the few that he had to his most treasured relationships. That coin acts as a reminder of the people who love me, who have sacrificed for me, and who support me on my journey. Since I travel a lot, I often pull out that coin and look at it. I allow the full weight of Michael's kind and loving words of friendship to wash over me.

Think of a memento that will remind you of how special you are and carry it with you for encouragement.

We become what we think about most. Affirm the state you want to be in and pretend you are already there. Now express your gratitude for each success as if it's already happened. For example, one of my mental affirmations is "I am naturally curious and always learning."

PHYSICAL AFFIRMATION:

MENTAL AFFIRMATION:

EMOTIONAL AFFIRMATION:

SPIRITUAL AFFIRMATION:

> "Shoot for the moon. Even if you miss, you'll land among the stars."
>
> -Les Brown

CREATE YOUR LONG VIEW

Create a long view of the dream destination to which your ticket will take you. Imagine using a pair of binoculars to focus on a long-term or lifetime goal. That destination is your BIG WHAT—what your journey is all about.

Here are some questions to help you determine your long view:

What will your life's great and unique contribution be?

_____

_____

_____

_____

At the end of your life, what will people say about you?

_____

_____

_____

_____

Be aware that negative naysayers drain your energy. Surround yourself with positive, powerful people who inspire you.

Your long view should be so emotional and so powerful that it ignites your soul and causes you to do things differently every day, week, month, and year. Write down your long view—your dream destination—and express it in such a way that it unlocks your passion to change and moves you to positive action every day.

P.S. Keep it simple.

"Words do two major things: They provide food for the mind and create light for understanding and awareness."

–Jim Rohn

"*To dream anything that you want to dream. That's the beauty of the human mind. To do anything that you want to do. That is the strength of the human will. To trust yourself to test your limits. That is the courage to succeed.*"
                                                            —Bernard Edmonds

"The real voyage of discovery consists not in seeking new landscapes, but in having new eyes."

-Marcel Proust

"Dreams and goals are the coming attractions in your life."

-JOSEPH CAMPBELL

5

MEANING

check your compass

You know where you want to go and you've got your ticket to ride. Now it's time to check your compass for guidance.

Each of us is born with a light that helps us know the difference between right and wrong. That internal compass—our conscience—ideally points us in the right direction. Sometimes that light grows dim. The compass no longer shows true north, and it stops directing us. Nothing is scarier than being hopelessly lost, aimlessly wandering without a sense of direction.

In our hurry-up, pressure-filled world, it's easy to get out of sync with your own internal compass—that voice inside you that lets you know when you're off track or, in my case, hurtling in the wrong direction. Take time daily to listen to your own voice. No matter what your current environment, you can learn to use your internal compass.

The important tool I used to set my internal compass was figuring out three things: my values, my purpose, and my long view.

MAPPING MY COURSE
MY VALUES

Become more AWARE of your values. Your values will influence nearly every choice you make and are part of your compass to keep you on the right path to your dream destination. Knowing what's important to you will help you stay steady and focused on your journey even when you hit potholes, roadblocks, and detours. If you don't know what you value, you just might end up adopting someone else's values.

Cindy Hunsinger, director of coaching for the Orange Duffel Bag Foundation, a nonprofit that does life plan coaching with at-risk youth, uses the next two exercises in her coaching practice to help people figure out values and gives a list of values for additional help:

Values List (partial)

Achievement	Caring	Connectedness
Acknowledgment	Challenge	Contribution/Giving
Appreciation	Charisma	Control
Artistic	Choice	Courage
Attractiveness	Clarity	Creativity
Authenticity	Collaboration	Decisiveness
Autonomy	Communication	Dedication
Balance	Community	Diligence
Beauty	Competition	Directness
Boldness	Connection	Effectiveness

Efficiency	Intimacy	Productivity
Elegance	Joy	Quality
Enjoyment	Knowledge	Quiet
Excitement	Leadership	Recognition
Exhilaration	Learning	Resiliency
Enthusiasm	Listening	Respect
Excellence	Love/Loving	Responsibility
Expertise	Loyalty	Risk/Risk-taking
Exploration	Moderation	Romance
Expression	Movement (Physical)	Security
Faith	Nature	Service
Fashion	Nurturing	Sharing
Fitness	Optimism	Spirituality
Focus	Order/Orderliness	Sports/Games
Friendship	Organization	Style/Fashion
Freedom	Originality	Success
Fun	Participation	To Be Known
Growth	Partnership	Tolerance
Helping	Passion	Tradition
Health/Well-being	Peace	Tranquillity
Honesty	Perseverance	Trust
Independence	Personal	Vitality
Influence	Development	Wisdom
Inspiration	Play/Playfulness	Zeal
Integrity	Power	
Interdependence	Process	

Write a description of a time in your life that felt really good—a peak moment, an achievement, a fun time—anything that meant a lot to you.

_____

_____

_____

_____

_____

_____

What values were present? *(You can reference the values listed on pages 48–49.)*

_____

_____

_____

_____

_____

_____

Another way to identify your values is to recall a time that did not feel good.

During my difficult childhood, I realized my values were vastly different from those of my family. Those hard times helped me clarify what values were important to me. A core value of my family was being TOUGH. But I realized that being KIND, TRUSTWORTHY, and RELIABLE were three of my main core values.

Write about a time in your life that was difficult or painful.

_____

_____

_____

_____

_____

_____

What values were NOT present? *(You can reference the values listed on pages 48–49.)*

_____

_____

_____

_____

TRAVEL TIP 151332

Make a collage on a sheet of paper or poster board illustrating what you value. Use photos, sayings, art, and words that are meaningful to you. Be creative. Keep your collage where you can see it, so that it reminds you to stay true to your path.

Based on your answers above, write down what you currently value or want to value and what the benefit of each value is:

VALUE:

Benefit:

VALUE:

Benefit:

VALUE:

Benefit:

VALUE:

Benefit:

Here are some additional exercises that might help you figure out what you stand for:

Name ten things that come easily for you. By thinking about what you enjoy and what you are good at, you will gain additional clues to your values.

1. _____

2. _____

3. _____

4. _____

5. _____

6. _____

7. _____

8. _____

9. _____

10. _____

Name ten people you admire and what you admire about them. Again, this exercise is intended to help you identify what values are important to you.

1. _____

2. _____

3. _____

4. _____

5. _____

6. _____

7. _____

8. _____

9. _____

10. _____

Now think about the specific values their lives represent that make you admire them.

If your home caught fire, what three things would you grab and why?

1. _____

2. _____

3. _____

If you won $1 million, what would you do with the money?

_____

_____

_____

_____

What keeps showing up? Look for the commonalities in your answers.

_____

_____

_____

Knowing how you rank your values will help you make better choices whenever you come to a fork in the road. Carefully consider your most important values whenever faced with a decision.

How do you know if you're in step with your values? If you feel happy and satisfied, you are likely in alignment with your values. When you feel anxious and off-kilter, your compass is telling you that you are heading in the wrong direction—or being led in the opposite direction of where you want to go.

MY PURPOSE

Now that you've identified your values, let them guide your journey. The values or principles that you choose to live by define you as a person and help you identify your life purpose. What is your purpose in life?

If you don't know what your purpose is, you'll likely feel lost, stuck, or unfulfilled. If you don't set your own goals according to your values and purpose, someone else might set them for you.

My purpose is to help unlock people's power to make positive changes in their lives, no matter their circumstances. If I hadn't grown up in a violent, abusive household and experienced huge setbacks like debilitating shoulder injuries and emotional meltdowns during college, I wouldn't be on this path.

Your purpose statement may be short and concise like mine, or you may want it to be a little longer. It is up to you.

Short version example:

- My purpose: *To help people unlock their ability to make positive changes.*

Longer version example:

• Orange Duffel Bag Foundation Coaching Director Cindy Hunsinger's purpose: *To live consciously and courageously, to resonate with love and compassion, to awaken authentic passion within others, and to leave this world in peace.*

My purpose in life is . . .

_____

_____

_____

_____

_____

_____

_____

MY LONG VIEW

Now you are ready to write about your long view—your future desired state. Think about what you've discovered thus far about your desires, values, passions, talents, and strengths. Those are the road signs that will help you map out your long view.

The following questions can help you express your long view:

What will your life's great and unique contribution be?

How do you want to make an impact?

"Whatever is true, whatever is noble, whatever is right, whatever
is pure, whatever is lovely, whatever is admirable—if anything
is excellent or praiseworthy—think about such things."

-Philippians 4:18

Imagine someone introducing you on a stage. What would that person say about you that would make you feel honored and proud of what you've done with your life?

_____

_____

_____

_____

_____

_____

_____

If you had the power to make a major difference in one arena, how would you want to influence change?

_____

_____

_____

At the end of your life, what will people say about you? What will your legacy be?

MY LONG VIEW:

TRAVEL TIP 151332

Keep it simple—just one to three sentences—and write it as if you've already arrived. Your long view should be concise and easy to remember. If you can't remember your long view statement, you've made it too complex.

TRAVEL TIP 151332

Understanding the WHY behind your long view increases your personal power. For example, my long view is to live an active life for as long as possible. Why is that my long view? Because I value being in good physical health. In order to accomplish my long view, I set a goal to lose forty pounds. Being clear on the why increases my commitment to my course. Everything we've done in this chapter is to make sure your compass is recalibrated and that you're in alignment with your values, purpose, and long view.

What is the reason behind your long view?

"The important thing is this: To be able at any moment to sacrifice what we are for what we could become."   -Charles DuBois

"*The best and most beautiful things in the world cannot be seen or even touched. They must be felt with the heart.*" 　　　　-Helen Keller

"The only way to change your story is to change what you believe about yourself. . . . Every time you change the main character of your story, the whole story changes to adapt to the new main character."

—DON MIGUEL RUIZ

pick your path and pack your bag

Now that you know where you want to go, you have your ticket to ride, and you've recalibrated your compass, how do you get there from here?

The choices you make on a daily basis will determine how well you stick to your chosen path. We literally make hundreds of choices each day without being aware of most or giving them much thought. Practice making good decisions even if it seems relatively unimportant in the scheme of things. And often it's the seemingly small choices that can have a dramatic impact on where you end up.

THERE ARE NO SMALL CHOICES

As a high school freshman, I set a goal of becoming a pro football player and an attorney. In order to reach those goals, I had to pick a path that would get me where I wanted to go.

To snag a scholarship, I knew I had to turn in consistently stellar performances on the football field, as well as study hard and make good grades throughout high school. And I didn't want to play football just anywhere. I wanted to play for a Division I school, so that I'd stand a good chance of making it into the pros. I also decided that just going to college wasn't enough. It had to be a school that was well-respected academically so that I'd stand the best chance of getting into law school. That was the path that I thought offered the clearest route out of the life of poverty I was living.

Learning to make good choices in the small things leads to making good choices when faced with the major things. Think of your mind and your ability to make choices as a gift.

I had to choose to be disciplined and focus on my homework on a daily basis even though there was often chaos going on around me.

I had to choose to ignore the temptation to take drugs or drink in order to numb myself to the pain of my life.

I had to choose to be dedicated to grueling, time-consuming workouts even though working as a busboy to support myself, going to school, playing ball, and running track exhausted me.

I had to choose not to give up hope when my knee got hurt when I was prepping for the all-star game in Las Vegas the summer after my senior year in high school.

Making those choices didn't come easy to me. Free will—the ability to make choices—is hardwired into all of us. It's at the core of our being. But we get tangled in our thinking and impaired in our ability to make good choices when we aren't allowed to exercise our free will in a safe, healthy environment.

Sometimes you are going to make the wrong choice. Making a misstep is rarely fatal. Do not allow yourself to be paralyzed by indecision if you make a wrong turn. When you get off the path, you'll need to take steps to get back on course.

Few people make it to their destination via a straight shot. You'll likely encounter detours, potholes, and road hazards along the way. On the surface, the football scholarship to the original school I was offered being given away and then my knee injury looked like complete and utter disasters. If those two events hadn't happened, I never would have landed at Georgia Tech and met Coach Bill Curry or Joan and Don Conkey, all of whom became surrogate parents to me. And because Georgia Tech emphasized the importance of the whole person and being well-rounded, I was empowered to let go of the negative baggage that was weighing me down.

Hope is a muscle. I chose to exercise that muscle and have faith that I had good directions. I hurdled the roadblock of fear.

The other big choice you face before you embark on your grand adventure is what to pack. The smart traveler knows to bring as little as possible but all the right stuff. Most of us tend to pack too much stuff. Extra baggage weighs you down and adds unnecessary stress. Ditch the excess baggage.

When I packed my orange duffel bag and left Las Vegas behind, I traveled light. I made a decision to let go of the past. I focused on the road ahead. Dwelling in the no-man's-land of the past often leads to regrets and sadness. It can completely derail you. Besides, you can be so busy looking back that you miss the beautiful scenery spread before you. I didn't want to miss any of the magnificent vistas my new future promised.

TRAVEL TIP
151332

Think about what choices you'll need to make on a daily basis to reach each goal and close each gap.

I forgave my mother for abandoning me.

You must pick your path with your end destination in mind.

MAPPING MY COURSE

What three key choices do you face right now that will determine
whether you meet your goals over the next twelve months? Write
down two or three choices that you are facing in each area.

PHYSICAL/BODY:

1. _____

2. _____

3. _____

MENTAL/MIND:

1. _____

2. _____

3. _____

EMOTIONAL/HEART:

1. _____

2. _____

3. _____

1.

2.

3.

What gaps (the space between where you are and where you want to be) do you need to close for each goal? (P.S. If there's no gap, there's no goal.) For example, here are my current goals and how I intend to close the gap, followed by space for you to record your own.

PHYSICAL/BODY:

- Sam's Goal: Lose weight—Go from 320 to 260 pounds by the end of the year.

- Close the Gap with diet and exercise.

- My Goal:

- I will Close the Gap by:

- My Goal:

_____

_____

- I will Close the Gap by:

_____

_____

- My Goal:

_____

_____

- I will Close the Gap by:

_____

_____

MENTAL/MIND:

- Sam's Goal: Become a successful author and speaker.
- Close the Gap by selling 1 million copies of *My Orange Duffel Bag*.

- My Goal:

_____

_____

- I will Close the Gap by:

_____

_____

- My Goal:

_____

_____

- I will Close the Gap by:

_____

_____

- My Goal:

_____

_____

- I will Close the Gap by:

_____

_____

FORGIVENESS IS A VITAL PART OF CHANGE— FORGIVING OTHERS AND YOURSELF.

 EMOTIONAL/HEART:

- Sam's Goal: Continue to deepen my relationship with Kim and our children.

- Close the Gap by spending quality time with Kim and by helping my kids feel secure and reach their potential.

- My Goal:

_____

_____

- I will Close the Gap by:

_____

_____

- My Goal:

_____

_____

- I will Close the Gap by:

_____

_____

- My Goal:

_____

_____

- I will Close the Gap by:

_____

_____

SPIRITUAL/SOUL:

- Sam's Goal: Get closer to God and do His will in all things.
- Close the Gap with regular prayer, scripture study, fasting, and service.

- My Goal:

_____

_____

- I will Close the Gap by:

_____

_____

- My Goal:

_____

_____

- I will Close the Gap by:

_____

_____

- My Goal:

_____

_____

- I will Close the Gap by:

_____

_____

Write down specific, actionable steps to accomplish your goals, steps you can track on a daily, weekly, and monthly basis. These goals are known as SMART goals: Specific, Measurable, Attainable, Realistic, and on a Timetable. I've found that the degree of my success in achieving my goals directly correlates to how detailed I am about the steps I plan to take toward each goal.

For example, for my physical goal of losing weight, I break down what steps I need to take on a daily, weekly, and monthly basis to accomplish the goal:

Each day I will do ninety minutes of cardio and will eliminate unhealthy snacks.

On a weekly basis, I will review my progress, my caloric intake, and the amount of time I spent exercising the previous week, and make any necessary adjustments to my workout and diet.

Each month I will map out my schedule to allow time for working out vigorously enough to achieve my weight loss goals.

Use the space below to write down the steps you will take to achieve your own SMART goals.

 PHYSICAL/BODY:

Goal:

_____

_____

Step I will take each day to accomplish it:

_____

_____

Step I will take each week to accomplish it:

_____

_____

Step I will take each month to accomplish it:

_____

_____

Goal:

_____

_____

Step I will take each day to accomplish it:

_____

_____

Step I will take each week to accomplish it:

_____

_____

Step I will take each month to accomplish it:

_____

_____

Goal:

_____

_____

Step I will take each day to accomplish it:

_____

_____

Step I will take each week to accomplish it:

_____

_____

Step I will take each month to accomplish it:

_____

_____

MENTAL/MIND:

Goal:

Step I will take each day to accomplish it:

Step I will take each week to accomplish it:

Step I will take each month to accomplish it:

Goal:

Step I will take each day to accomplish it:

TRAVEL TIP 151332

Few people make it to their destination via a straight shot. You'll likely encounter detours, potholes, and road hazards along the way. Sometimes you are going to make the wrong choice. It is rarely fatal. Do not allow yourself to be paralyzed by regret or indecision. Learn from the experience and get back on track.

Step I will take each week to accomplish it:

_____

_____

Step I will take each month to accomplish it:

_____

_____

Goal:

_____

_____

Step I will take each day to accomplish it:

_____

_____

Step I will take each week to accomplish it:

Step I will take each month to accomplish it:

 EMOTIONAL/HEART:

Goal:

Step I will take each day to accomplish it:

Step I will take each week to accomplish it:

Step I will take each month to accomplish it:

Goal:

_____

_____

Step I will take each day to accomplish it:

_____

_____

Step I will take each week to accomplish it:

_____

_____

Step I will take each month to accomplish it:

_____

_____

Goal:

_____

_____

Step I will take each day to accomplish it:

_____

_____

Step I will take each week to accomplish it:

_____

_____

Step I will take each month to accomplish it:

_____

_____

SPIRITUAL/SOUL:

Goal:

_____

_____

Step I will take each day to accomplish it:

_____

_____

Step I will take each week to accomplish it:

_____

_____

Step I will take each month to accomplish it:

_____

_____

Goal:

_____

_____

Step I will take each day to accomplish it:

_____

_____

Step I will take each week to accomplish it:

_____

_____

Step I will take each month to accomplish it:

_____

_____

Goal:

_____

_____

Step I will take each day to accomplish it:

_____

_____

Step I will take each week to accomplish it:

_____

_____

Step I will take each month to accomplish it:

_____

_____

Hold yourself accountable. Use a calendar, these pages, or part 2 of this book, *Mapping My Journey*, to stay on top of each goal and action step. I use my goal book to do so, and I keep the big goals and the gaps on a bookmark that I can look at every day.

What threatens to block your chosen path or slow you down?

_____

_____

_____

_____

_____

_____

_____

_____

TRAVEL TIP 151332

Prepare for a successful journey by anticipating possible problems and thinking through solutions. For example, after getting a 2.7 GPA my first semester at Georgia Tech, I realized that I needed extra help academically. I found out that through the athletic department's total person program I was eligible for free tutoring. I never missed a tutoring session in vital classes, and I graduated with honors.

Now that you've picked your path, it's time to pack your bag. Experienced travelers rely on a packing list.

What will you need on your journey and when you arrive at your destination? Although all my orange duffel bag had in it when I arrived at Georgia Tech was a few T-shirts, some underwear, and an extra pair of jeans, I had learned by that point to pack my bag with some important items both physically and metaphorically.

Here are some of the things I take with me on my journey:

Books that contain uplifting messages and expand my horizons.

Music lifts my mood, so I always carry favorites with me and listen to them.

My Roadmap, so that I can examine my path, track my progress, journal my thoughts about any roadblocks I encounter as well as the victories along the way, and count my many blessings.

Positive affirmations to help me stay on the right path. If I'm struggling with negative thoughts, I find sayings, scriptures, and encouraging quotes that address my issues. I write them on index cards and memorize them, replacing my negative thinking with positives that help me along my journey.

I keep mementos (objects that remind you of something or someone in your past) that illustrate how far I've come.

Write down your packing list. What you choose to pack should be tools and strategies you need to reach your dream destination, like the ones I've shared. Note beside each item on your packing list how it will aid you on your journey.

1. _____
2. _____
3. _____
4. _____
5. _____
6. _____
7. _____
8. _____
9. _____
10. _____

"Life is not easy for any of us. But what of that? We must have perseverance and, above all, confidence in ourselves. We must believe that we are gifted for something and that this thing must be attained."

-Marie Curie

"Once you perceive that you have choices, you have the choice to live your own light. Dance with it. Listen to it and follow it."

—Carlos Santana

"We gain strength, and courage, and confidence by each experience in which we really stop to look fear in the face. . . . We must do that which we think we cannot."   —Eleanor Roosevelt

"When we feel love and kindness toward others, it not only makes others feel loved and cared for, but it helps us also to develop inner happiness and peace."

-THE DALAI LAMA

choose your traveling companions and guides carefully

Choosing the right people to accompany you on your journey can make it more successful and fun. The wrong traveling companions can impede your progress and get you way off track.

Surround yourself with positive, powerful people. You'll be amazed at how much you'll be elevated and supercharged—and how much easier it will be to accomplish your goals.

When you don't have good boundaries with people who drag you down, the temptation to think of yourself as a victim without choices becomes stronger and stronger. Failing to recognize that you have choices leads you to resign yourself to your current position in life.

Think about each of your closest relationships. Is that person helping you along your path or is he or she holding you back?

In other words: Hang out with eagles and you'll soar. Hang out with pigs and you'll stink.

MAPPING MY COURSE

Who will help you on your journey? **We all need guides. We need many friends and mentors to help us along the path to our best selves. Keep your eyes open for those special people whom you trust and who know the best routes, the shortcuts, and the fun side trips that you'd never discover without them by your side.**

Write the name of someone you know and admire.

_____

What made you pick this person?

_____

_____

_____

_____

_____

_____

_____

"Learn everything you can, anytime you can, from anyone you can—there will always come a time when you will be grateful you did."

-Sarah Caldwell

What characteristics attract you to that person?

_____

_____

_____

_____

_____

Do you share any of these characteristics with the person you admire?

_____

_____

_____

_____

_____

Could this person serve as a guide in one of the below areas?

Write down one or two positive and caring people who serve (or could serve) as your guide in each of these areas. A guide can help expose you to a path you might not otherwise have considered and can help you navigate roadblocks.

PHYSICAL/BODY:

_____

_____

_____

_____

MENTAL/MIND:

_____

_____

_____

_____

EMOTIONAL/HEART:

_____

_____

_____

_____

SPIRITUAL/SOUL:

_____

_____

_____

_____

Initiate one-on-one time with each person this week. Share your goals in the area where you want that person's support. Be respectful of schedules, but be clear that you'd like a relationship. Establish regular contact, whether it's a virtual relationship or you're able to meet in person.

Write down the name of a friend or family member who encourages you in each of the areas listed.

PHYSICAL/BODY:

_____

_____

_____

_____

MENTAL/MIND:

_____

_____

_____

_____

EMOTIONAL/HEART:

_____

_____

TRAVEL TIP 151332

If someone close to you is a negative influence, choose to minimize that person's importance in your life. Whenever the person who drags you down starts talking, practice seeing that person in your mind as a tiny being the size of a housefly. It's a funny visual, but this exercise will gradually help you to steel yourself against the onslaught of negativity.

_____

_____

SPIRITUAL/SOUL:

_____

_____

_____

_____

Spend the bulk of your free time with these encouragers.

Are there people in your life who you've allowed to block your forward progress?

A lot of people make this mistake. They surround themselves with people who don't support the positive changes they want to make. These toxic people are emotional vampires who suck the life energy out of you and kill your goals and dreams.

If you find yourself being drained by someone, give yourself permission to set a safe boundary with that person. We don't always

Learn to forgive and let go. Feeling resentment and bitterness is like taking poison and expecting the person you harbor hatred toward to die. I forgave my mother for abandoning me and reconciled with her. We formed a safe, caring relationship and enjoyed each other's company for several years before her death.

have control over who is in our lives, but we do have control over how we let them influence us. I had no choice about what family I was born into, but once I enrolled in college, I limited my contact with my family, because I knew our values were too different. Bad coaches, difficult bosses, mean classmates, or grumbling coworkers can make achieving your goals difficult. When someone in your life is negative, find ways to minimize his or her influence on you and actively seek out positive people to reduce the harm these toxic bullies cause. Give yourself permission to hang up the phone if someone is abusive, to remove yourself from that person's presence, to say no to demands on you.

> "Love doesn't make the world go 'round; love is what makes the ride worthwhile."
>
> -Franklin P. Jones

How can you limit that person's negative influence on your life and set good boundaries?

_____

_____

_____

_____

_____

_____

One way to attract more positive people into your life and gain the strength to eliminate the ones who are holding you back is to work on loving yourself enough to recognize that you deserve the support and the joy that comes from having people in your life who are uplifting. You cannot accept love and give love if you don't love yourself.

How do you affirm your love for yourself? Check your self-talk. Is it positive or negative?

Here's a good test: Think about some of the things you tell yourself. Would you want to be friends with a person who said those things to you on a regular basis? If the answer is no, go back to page 38 and review your list of positive attributes.

Write down ten things that you like most about yourself right now.

1. _____

2. _____

3. _____

4. _____

5. _____

6. _____

7. _____

8. _____

9. _____

10. _____

Look at this list on a daily basis if you struggle with negative self-talk.

Another way is to be an encourager to other people, too. Is there someone to whom you could serve as a guide?

_____

One of the best ways to learn is to share our knowledge with others.

Get in the habit of offering a compliment or a positive thought to someone each day. Too often, we focus on problems or what's going wrong and rarely take time to offer praise and encouragement. Let's change that.

"The great tragedy of life is not that men perish, but that they cease to love."

—W. Somerset Maugham

"*Love is a choice you make from moment to moment.*"

-Barbara De Angelis

"How wonderful it is that nobody need wait a single moment before starting to improve the world."

-Anne Frank

CHANGE

enjoy the journey

To be a good traveler, you've got to be adaptable. Weather and schedules change. The food may be different from what you're used to. You may encounter delays or detours, or the route you've mapped out may be blocked unexpectedly.

Some of the best things that have happened in my life resulted from what initially looked like a roadblock. I met my wife, Kim, when I got sent to a different place on my church mission after initially struggling with my first assignment. I earned a scholarship with Georgia Tech and met Coach Bill Curry, who became my lifelong mentor, because my scholarship to what I considered my dream school was given to someone else.

Throughout this book, you've been working on creating your Roadmap for your life. One of the most important lessons is to understand that your map likely won't take you exactly where you think you want to go. Your course will take shifts and turns. Embrace change and figure out how to make the most of the unexpected.

MAPPING MY COURSE

Don't let a detour or a roadblock completely derail your journey. Learn to see changes in your path as opportunities rather than barriers. Sometimes the side trips give us wonderful, unexpected pleasures.

Figure out how to adapt.

What is a roadblock you are facing right now?

_____

_____

_____

_____

_____

_____

_____

_____

_____

_____

"No person is your friend who demands your silence, or denies your right to grow."

-Alice Walker

TRAVEL TIP 151332

Make adjustments to your course as needed. Celebrate your victories whenever you reach specific mile markers along your journey. Remember, if you shoot for the moon, you'll land among the stars.

Write down three possible routes around the roadblock.

1.

2.

3.

"It is not the strongest of the species that survive, nor the most intelligent, but the ones most responsive to change."

-Charles Darwin

Now allow your imagination to kick in. What are three good things that you think could come from taking an unexpected route?

1.

2.

3.

Write down some unexpected benefits of a change in your course that has occurred. Reflect on the good that came from something you might have originally thought was a negative shift in your life. Take time to appreciate the unexpected gifts of your journey.

If you tackle the boldest goal on your list—even if it seems virtually impossible—name five good things that might happen as a result. I didn't achieve some of the wildest goals that I originally set for myself, but the act of mapping out those goals led me to amazing experiences and new goals.

1. _____

_____

_____

2. _____

_____

_____

3. _____

_____

_____

4. _____

_____

_____

5. _____

_____

_____

"I can't change the direction of the wind, but I can adjust my sails to always reach my destination."   -Jimmy Dean

"*Education is the most powerful weapon which you can use to change the world.*"

-Nelson Mandela

"Develop an attitude of gratitude, and give thanks for everything that happens to you, knowing that every step forward is a step toward achieving something bigger and better than your current situation."

-BRIAN TRACY

share your adventures

When you go on an incredible journey, what's the first thing you do when you arrive home? You share your adventures with others—your stories, your experiences, your lessons learned, and your photos from the trip.

> *"The single greatest thing you can do to change your life today would be to start being grateful for what you have right now."*
>
> -Oprah Winfrey

One of the most important things you can do as you move forward on your path is share your adventures.

Doing that helps you to be grateful for the traveling companions and guides who accompanied you. It reminds you of all the wonderful

places you've been and the excitement you felt when you overcame
hardships along the way.

MAPPING MY COURSE

Think about your journey thus far. What are you grateful for on your
journey? Write down as many things as you can. Your gratitude list
can include people, things, places, and experiences. Be specific.
Think of each of the four areas of a whole human being (physical/
body, mental/mind, emotional/heart, and spiritual/soul) as you com-
pose your list.

_____

_____

_____

_____

_____

_____

_____

When you are filled with gratitude for those who helped you
along the path, the view from wherever you are looks so much better. Over the next week, spend the first few minutes of your day ap-
preciating the view, the experiences, and the people you meet. End
each day the same way. When you practice an attitude of gratitude,
you'll find more and more things to appreciate along your journey.
Notice how your spirits lift as you read over your gratitude lists.

- Look for and find something to be grateful for every day.

- Express your gratitude for your blessings every day.

- Record things that you are learning.

- Write about your accomplishments and struggles.

- Discover the joy in the simple things.

- Take time to prioritize your activities and responsibilities.

- Look up. Set your sights on the things that matter most. See beyond your horizon. Try to imagine where you'll be in a year, two years, five years, and ten years. Pick a beautiful place and picture it in detail.

Take time to renew, refresh, fuel up for yourself each day. It's difficult to give to others from a place of emptiness.

What "rocks your world"?

What inspires you or gives you energy?

_____

_____

_____

_____

_____

_____

_____

_____

_____

_____

_____

_____

_____

_____

_____

_____

_____

Continue the work you've done here in the third part of this book, *My Life* (page 135), and use it as your Gratitude Journal.

> "At times our own light goes out and is rekindled by a spark from another person. Each of us has cause to think with deep gratitude of those who have lighted the flame within us."   —Albert Schweitzer

"*Gratitude makes sense of our past, brings peace for today, and creates a vision for tomorrow.*"

-Sarah Caldwell

"Man, it's good

to be someone.

Put an end to all our

doubt and live our

lives out loud."

ARTIST/SONGWRITER
ROB THOMAS

You've discovered for yourself how writing down your goals in each of these four areas—physical, mental, emotional, and spiritual—will propel you far on your journey. You've already begun mapping your path to radical change in part one, *7 Rules for the Road*. Now use these pages to map out your journey in greater detail and continue charting your course.

We've divided this part of the book into the four areas. Use the first page of each section to write down exactly where you are in that area right now. I call this taking a personal inventory. Be brutally honest with yourself. You may not like what you see written in black-and-white.

Then write down a few key items in each area that you want to change over the next twelve months. Don't write down too many goals or you'll get overwhelmed. Next, for each goal write a compelling reason to accomplish it. Finally, write down for each goal how you will accomplish it and by when. For it to be a goal, you must be able to measure your success.

For the first two weeks after you write down your goals, read what you've written for at least fifteen minutes each morning. Visualize yourself being successful in each area. Practice success in your mind. After a few weeks, you may choose to cut out the first page.

Coach Curry didn't want me to dwell on anything negative, so he had me tear out the pages that had my personal inventory and throw them away. If, like mine, your initial inventory is painful, you can cut it out of this book. You may even want to burn it. This physical act helps you focus on the future—not on past shortcomings or failures.

Every day, positively embrace what you want, why you want it, and how and when you will get it. Affirm your success in each area and keep working hard. If you feel comfortable, share your goals with a trusted friend, who can encourage you.

Write down exactly where you are right now in the four key areas that make you who you are. This exercise will give you your starting point.

Don't hold back. Now is the time to be real with yourself.

PHYSICAL/BODY: Where am I right now?

What do you want to change in this area? Name two to three specific goals you would like to accomplish in the next twelve months. Be as specific as possible. Don't just say, for example, "I want to lose weight." Notice how much more power is in a statement like, "I want to lose 50 pounds and be fit enough to be active with my wife and kids, so I can live longer and have more fun with those I love most."

Why do you want to accomplish these goals?

How will you measure your success in each goal, and by when will you achieve it?

Goal 1:

Goal 2:

Goal 3:

I will accomplish

Goal 1 by doing these things:

_____

_____

_____

_____

The Big WHY:

_____

_____

By the following date:

_____

Goal 2 by doing these things:

_____

_____

_____

_____

The Big WHY:

_____

_____

119

By the following date:

Goal 3 by doing these things:

The Big WHY:

By the following date:

Commit to these goals by signing your name:

Name

Date

MENTAL/MIND: Where am I right now?

What do you want to change in this area? Name two to three specific goals you would like to accomplish in the next twelve months. Be as specific as possible.

Why do you want to accomplish these goals?

How will you measure your success in each goal, and by when will you achieve it?

Goal 1:

_____

_____

_____

_____

Goal 2:

_____

_____

_____

_____

Goal 3:

_____

_____

_____

_____

I will accomplish

Goal 1 by doing these things:

_____

_____

_____

_____

The Big WHY:

_____

_____

By the following date:

_____

Goal 2 by doing these things:

_____

_____

_____

_____

The Big WHY:

_____

_____

By the following date:

Goal 3 by doing these things:

The Big WHY:

By the following date:

Commit to these goals by signing your name:

Name

Date

EMOTIONAL/HEART: Where am I right now?

What do you want to change in this area? Name two to three specific goals you would like to accomplish in the next twelve months. Be as specific as possible.

Why do you want to accomplish these goals?

How will you measure your success in each goal, and by when will you achieve it?

Goal 1:

_____

_____

_____

_____

Goal 2:

_____

_____

_____

Goal 3:

_____

_____

_____

I will accomplish

Goal 1 by doing these things:

_____

_____

_____

_____

The Big WHY:

_____

_____

By the following date:

_____

Goal 2 by doing these things:

_____

_____

_____

_____

The Big WHY:

_____

_____

By the following date:

_____

Goal 3 by doing these things:

_____

_____

_____

_____

The Big WHY:

_____

_____

By the following date:

_____

Commit to these goals by signing your name:

_____

Name

_____

Date

SPIRITUAL/SOUL: Where am I right now?

What do you want to change in this area? Name two to three specific goals you would like to accomplish in the next twelve months. Be as specific as possible.

Why do you want to accomplish these goals?

How will you measure your success in each goal, and by when will you achieve it?

Goal 1:

_____

_____

_____

_____

Goal 2:

_____

_____

_____

_____

Goal 3:

_____

_____

_____

I will accomplish

Goal 1 by doing these things:

_____

_____

_____

_____

_____

_____

The Big WHY:

_____

_____

By the following date:

_____

Goal 2 by doing these things:

_____

_____

_____

_____

_____

The Big WHY:

_____

_____

By the following date:

_____

Goal 3 by doing these things:

_____

_____

_____

_____

_____

The Big WHY:

_____

_____

By the following date:

_____

Commit to these goals by signing your name:

_____

Name

_____

Date

"You'll fail at 100% of the goals you don't set."

-Mark Victor Hansen

"One life,

but we're not

the same.

We get to carry

each other."

ARTISTS: U2 AND MARY J. BLIGE
SONGWRITERS: U2

MY LIFE

Throughout my journey, I've taken time each day to write down what I am grateful for and whom I'm grateful for.

Sometimes I think of little things that I might be tempted to overlook. Sometimes I write down big things that make my heart swell with overwhelming thanks. The list of people who have made a difference in my life expands all the time.

Now a wealth of research has shown that people who regularly record what they are thankful for and review what they have written on a daily basis tend to be more satisfied in life. Your mind is powerful, and if you dwell on the good, you'll soon notice your spirits improve and you'll find that your attitude becomes more and more positive.

This one simple act can make an enormous difference in your life. On and off throughout my life, I have struggled with depression, anger, and sadness. My gratitude list offers a powerful antidote to these negative thoughts.

On the following pages, continue the work you began in Rule 7 and write down what you are grateful for and whom you are grateful for. You'll find so many things and people to be grateful for that you'll likely need another book to record your daily list. I break mine into the four categories.

Some people record answers to prayers. Others write down people who help them and events that touch their hearts. Be specific. I like to read my list at the end of the day, so that these people and things are the last things I think about as I go to sleep.

"Gratitude is not only the greatest of virtues, but the parent of all others."

-Cicero

"*Be who you are and say what you feel because those who mind don't matter and those who matter don't mind.*"   -Dr. Seuss

"The key to change . . . is to let go of fear."   -Roseanne Cash

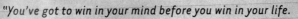

"*You've got to win in your mind before you win in your life.*

-John Addison

MY FINAL QUESTION IS:
ARE YOU THERE YET?

Hint: The answer is no. When you think you have arrived, you are in trouble. Stay true to the great journey mapped out for you. Remember and review the 7 *Rules for the Road* often. I can't wait to see where my orange duffel bag goes with me next.

Celebrate the journey,
Sam Bracken

P.S. Share your adventures at www.MyOrangeDuffelBag.com or on our Facebook page. I'd love to hear from you and learn about your progress.

ABOUT THE AUTHORS

SAM BRACKEN is the author of *My Orange Duffel Bag*. He serves as the national spokesman for the Orange Duffel Bag Foundation. He is also a general manager of FranklinCovey Media Publishing, a division of the world's foremost training and leadership development company, operating in 147 countries. A member of the National Speakers Association, Sam graduated Georgia Tech with honors and received his MBA from Brigham Young University's Marriott School of Management. He and his wife, Kim, live in the Rocky Mountains with their four children.

Sam is available for select readings and lectures. To inquire about a possible appearance, please visit www.rhspeakers.com or call 212-572-2013. For group or corporate coaching and training based on Sam's 7 *Rules for the Road*, please contact him at sbracken@mac.com.

> www.facebook.com/pages/SamBracken/208860949175067
> ?sk=wall@SamBracken67; twitter.com/#!/sambracken67
> SBracken67; www.youtube.com/user/sbracken67

ECHO GARRETT, a journalist with thirty years' experience, is the author of *Why Don't They Just Get a Job? One Couple's Mission to End Poverty in Their Community*, *Dream No Little Dreams*, and several other books. Formerly editor in chief of *Atlanta Woman*, Echo has been published in more than seventy-five national publications and has appeared on *Good Morning America*, CNBC, CNN, and NY-1. She holds a journalism degree from Auburn University. Echo and her husband, Kevin Garrett, a photographer who contributed most of the images in this book and *My Orange Duffel Bag*, have two sons, Caleb and Connor, and reside in metro Atlanta. She cofounded the Orange Duffel Bag Foundation and works to support its mission.

To book Echo for a speaking engagement, contact her at echo@echogarrett.com

> www.echogarrett.com
> Facebook: www.facebook.com/pages/Echo-
> Garrett/155148734571077?sk=wall
> Twitter: @echogarrett; twitter.com/#!/echogarrett

> MyOrangeDuffelBag.com
> Facebook: www.facebook.com/pages/My-Orange-Duffel-Bag-A-
> Journey-To-Radical-Change/166020844367

BE THAT ONE TO HELP JUST ONE

The Orange Duffel Bag Foundation—a 501(c)(3) nonprofit cofounded by Sam Bracken and Echo Garrett—is dedicated to providing professional life coaching, training, and advocacy for youth in foster care and at-risk and homeless youth to help them become self-reliant. Join us in bringing hope, meaning, and change to our at-risk youth ages twelve to twenty-four. A portion of the proceeds from *My Roadmap* goes to support the Orange Duffel Bag Foundation (ODBF). Here's how you can help with our mission:

1. With your cell phone, you can donate $10 by texting the word ORANGE to this number: 85944. Reply YES when prompted and your donation will be charged to your phone bill.

2. Donate $500 to sponsor a case of *My Orange Duffel Bag* books, which will allow us to give them to a group home for youth in foster care. Reading the book is the first step on their journey to radical change.

3. A $2,500 donation provides an at-risk youth with our full twelve-week professional life coaching. Upon graduation, each young person receives an orange duffel bag filled with useful items and has access to our family of ODBF advocates, caring adults who assist the ODBF graduate on his or her journey.

www.OrangeDuffelBagFoundation.org

Toll-free in United States, call 1-800-598-5150

Email: orangeduffelbagfoundation@gmail.com

Follow us on Facebook:

http://www.facebook.com/pages/Orange-Duffel-Bag-Foundation/
138001609577884

Twitter: @ODBFoundation

http://twitter.com/#!/ODBFoundation